FAT-BURNING
FOOD GUIDE

THIS FOOD GUIDE IS DESIGNED TO PROVIDE YOU WITH EVERYTHING YOU NEED TO USE FOOD TO TURN YOUR BODY INTO A LEAN, MEAN FAT-BURNING

WELCOME TO THE CHALEAN EXTREME™ FAT-BURNING FOOD GUIDE.

I subscribe to a diet that is high in protein, very low in sugar, and moderately low in carbohydrates and fat. This nutrition/food "prescription" is my ultimate health "cure" for your body. Simply follow the plan and your body will not only become healthier but also leaner and stronger.

I stress a high-protein diet because protein will fuel and support your muscles. But don't confuse this with an Atkins-type diet—it's a balanced diet with the right protein. I call it "high protein" because many people who exercise don't eat enough protein. By increasing your protein intake, you will fuel muscle building, which creates a faster metabolism. In other words, this high-protein diet, which aids muscle development, will result in weight loss and fat loss, even as you consume more calories!

I cannot stress enough how important choosing the right foods and eating a nutritionally balanced diet are for this life-changing journey! For us to create the lean bodies we desire, we need the best fuel possible because we have to add muscle—and "Muscle Burns Fat!" Think of your body as a well-oiled machine—if you don't provide it with top-of-the line fuel, in the appropriate amounts, the likelihood of your body getting you to where you need to go is slim to none.

If you learn what to eat, when to eat, and why food is fuel, you will add that muscle to burn fat more efficiently, improve your energy, increase your metabolism, and experience your own extreme transformation. Here I have outlined my nutritional philosophy, provided many heart-smart and body-friendly recipes, and highlighted some optimal nutritional habits that you can adopt for the rest of your life. Following this guide is sure to change the way your body looks and the way you feel about yourself!

Yours in Health and Happiness,

Chalene Johnson

TABLE OF CONTENTS

06 PHILOSOPHY AND GUIDELINES

08 THE LEAN-PHASING APPROACH TO EATING

11 BASICS OF THE FAT-BURNING FOOD GUIDE

17 WHEN TO EAT, WHAT TO DRINK

20 RECIPES FOR LIFE

22 BURN BREAKFASTS

33 PUSH BREAKFASTS

36 LEAN BREAKFASTS

41 BURN LUNCHES

52 PUSH LUNCHES

54 LEAN LUNCHES

59 BURN DINNERS

74 PUSH DINNERS

78 LEAN DINNERS

83 BURN SNACKS

92 PUSH SNACKS

93 LEAN SNACKS

94 SALAD BAR

97 LEAN FOR LIFE MAINTENANCE PROGRAM

100 TIPS FOR DINING OUT

PHILOSOPHY AND GUIDELINES

You should be eating 5 times a day, specifically 3 meals and 2 snacks that have the proper balance of proteins, carbohydrates, and fats. It has been proven that eating 3 meals and 2 snacks every 2 to 3 hours helps maximize your body's fat-burning abilities. Research also shows that lowering your sugar and carbohydrate intake can decrease your fat stores. When you go through periods of more than 3 hours without food, you actually increase your fat stores and slow your metabolism. That way of eating must end today!

The suggested daily intake of calories for men and women to lose weight varies. Larger or fitter individuals should start at the higher end of the calorie range, while smaller or less fit individuals should start at the lower end of the calorie range.

See the table below to figure out where you fall on the calorie spectrum.

WOMEN'S
ESTIMATED CALORIE NEEDS FOR WEIGHT LOSS

CURRENT WEIGHT	ESTIMATED CALORIE NEEDS FOR WEIGHT LOSS
100–120 pounds	1,200 calories/day
121–150 pounds	1,300 calories/day
151–180 pounds	1,400 calories/day
181+ pounds	1,500 calories/day

MEN'S
ESTIMATED CALORIE NEEDS FOR WEIGHT LOSS

CURRENT WEIGHT	ESTIMATED CALORIE NEEDS FOR WEIGHT LOSS
130–150 pounds	1,400 calories/day
151–170 pounds	1,500 calories/day
171–190 pounds	1,600 calories/day
191+ pounds	1,700 calories/day

You can calculate your specific calorie needs with the Caloric Needs Calculator at **TeamBeachbody.com**. *JOIN THE TEAM BEACHBODY® CLUB NOW TO ENJOY THIS AND MANY OTHER BENEFITS!*

In this guide, you will find breakfasts, lunches, and dinners that equal approximately 1,000 calories per day. Based on your calorie needs, add snacks to total your daily calorie goal. Snacks are vital components of your nutrition plan.

If you don't need to lose weight, you may want to add 1 to 2 ounces of lean protein to your meals or snacks.

THE LEAN-PHASING APPROACH TO EATING

The Fat-Burning Food Plan is also broken down into phases. The first month is the Burn Phase, the second month is the Push Phase, the third month is the Lean Phase, and then you will move on to more of a maintenance phase—Lean for Life.

The good news is that this nutrition plan will become more liberal as you progress from one phase to the next. In other words, you will be increasing your calorie intake and allowing yourself more "treats" as you continue the plan. This philosophy of increasing calories is based on the fact that your metabolism will be increasing as you increase your lean body mass. Research shows that redundant food plans lead to boredom and failure, but with the Fat-Burning Food Plan, you will continually add more diversity and intrigue to your daily meals and snacks.

You should be eating 5 times a day—3 meals and 2 snacks.

BURN PHASE

During this first phase of the nutrition plan, you will choose meals from the Burn meal and snack lists to hit the calorie range suggested on page 7. These meals and snacks are low in refined carbs and fat and also rich in lean protein and vegetables.

PUSH PHASE

During this second phase of the Fat-Burning Food Plan, you will enjoy increased portion sizes of the Burn Meals. You will find new Push meals and snacks to choose from. Choose 1 Breakfast, 1 Lunch, 1 Dinner, and 1 Snack from the Push Phase menu each week. These meals are slightly higher in calories, mostly in the form of protein.

See the example on the right and enjoy selections from the Burn menu the other 3 days of the week.

FOR EXAMPLE, YOUR PUSH PHASE WEEK WILL LOOK LIKE THIS:

MONDAY	TUESDAY	WEDNESDAY	THURSDAY
Burn Breakfast	Push Breakfast	Burn Breakfast	Burn Breakfast
Burn Snack	Burn Snack	Push Snack	Burn Snack
Burn Lunch	Burn Lunch	Burn Lunch	Push Lunch
Burn Snack	Burn Snack	Burn Snack	Burn Snack
Push Dinner	Burn Dinner	Burn Dinner	Burn Dinner

YOU GET THE PICTURE!

Remember that in the Push Phase **you are eating the increased portion sizes of the** Burn Meals **and now enjoying** 4 Push Meals **a week.**

LEAN PHASE

You're eating increased portions of the Burn Meals. You can also choose 4 NEW Push Meals and 4 NEW Lean Meals. Remember, "meals" also include snacks—and you are ideally choosing 1 Breakfast, 1 Lunch, 1 Dinner, and 1 Snack from the different phases.

A SAMPLE LEAN PHASE WEEK OF EATING MAY LOOK LIKE THE FOLLOWING:

MONDAY	TUESDAY	WEDNESDAY	THURSDAY
Burn Breakfast	Burn Breakfast	Push Breakfast	Lean Breakfast
Burn Snack	Burn Snack	Burn Snack	Burn Snack
Burn Lunch	Burn Lunch	Lean Lunch	Push Lunch
Push Snack	Lean Snack	Burn Snack	Burn Snack
Lean Dinner	Push Dinner	Burn Dinner	Burn Dinner

LEAN FOR LIFE

Refer to page 97 to read more about this maintenance phase.

If at any point in the program you hit a plateau (more than 2 weeks), go back to the previous phase in the diet. This will ensure that you are not increasing calories faster than your body's metabolism is increasing. If you need to increase your energy or up your calorie intake, try adding 1 to 2 ounces of protein to your snack(s) or meal(s).

BASICS OF THE FAT-BURNING FOOD GUIDE

ChaLEAN Extreme is different from other programs. I want you to understand not just what to eat but why you overeat and why so many of us struggle with making healthy food choices, even when we know right from wrong. I have created a motivational audio program to help address the reasons we eat, other than hunger, and to help get a handle on the emotional triggers that cause so many people to eat when they are not hungry.

Before you begin, I want you to have a basic understanding of how nutrition works with your body to help you experience the full power of healthy eating.

PROTEIN, CARBOHYDRATES, **and** FAT **are the main elements that make up the food we eat. The meals and snacks in this Fat-Burning Food Guide are high in protein, low in carbs, and low in fat.**

By following this plan, you will be eating lean proteins and reducing the amount of starchy carbohydrates you eat (for example: breads, pastas, cereals, etc.). This will help you maximize your results, and your body will start burning stored fat as fuel.

PROTEIN

Protein helps maintain lean muscle mass and provides energy for your body to build and repair your muscles, bones, and tissues. To get the most out of protein, it is important to know which proteins are beneficial to your body.

BEEF: Look for "grass fed" or "free range" beef. This type of beef comes from a smaller, leaner cow that feeds on high-protein grasses like alfalfa and rye. This cow's beef is lower in cholesterol and fat. This type of cow "exercises"—it roams the range and eats when it's hungry. Avoid "corn fed" or "aged" beef with high marbling or fat. While it may be extra tasty, it's loaded with fat and cholesterol.

CHICKEN: Eat "free range" birds that are hormone- and chemical-free. Avoid birds that have been confined to a cage, injected with hormones, and force-fed to fatten them up. Try to eat white-meat chicken, like skinless chicken breast.

FISH: Eat the freshest, most natural fish available. If these are farm-raised (not pond-raised), they are raised in a more natural habitat, which allows for a constant flow of water and a natural diet. Avoid "pond raised" fish. These types of hatcheries tend to be full of algae and bacteria. Artificial coloring and preservatives are sometimes added to make these fish more visually appealing.

VEGETARIANS

Many "vegetarians" still eat eggs, dairy, and fish, all of which are excellent sources of protein. These "vegetarians" rarely have problems getting plenty of protein in their diets.

However, there are plenty of protein options available. Some major sources of proteins are whole grains and legumes. Beans, peas, and lentils are loaded with protein and fiber (as well as carbohydrates) and are staple foods for many vegans. You can also choose tofu, tempeh, and veggie burgers.

Many other foods have protein in lesser amounts. These include nuts, seeds, many grains, and most veggies. Accessorizing your diet with these foods makes it easy to get plenty of protein.

CARBOHYDRATES

The amount and type of carbohydrates in your diet could be the most important factors when it comes to weight loss and fat reduction; and carbohydrates are not created equal. Carbohydrates need to be eaten with care, as there is a distinction between "good" carbs and their "bad" counterparts.

When carbohydrates are consumed, they are broken down into sugars and are absorbed into the bloodstream as glucose, or blood sugar. This sugar feeds our brains and gives our bodies energy; however, too much sugar at once, or the wrong kind of sugar, cannot be efficiently processed by the body and will be stored as fat. However, eating too many "good" carbs can contribute to slow or no weight loss.

HEALTHY CARBS: Much has been said these days about "low glycemic" carbohydrates. "Low glycemic" means that they are released into the bloodstream at a slower rate, which gives more long-term energy and reduced blood sugar and insulin spikes. The best carbohydrates are fiber-rich fruits like apples, vegetables, whole grains, low-fat dairy, beans, and legumes.

UNHEALTHY CARBS: The human body does not process refined "high glycemic" carbohydrates well. They are quickly broken down into simple sugar and, therefore, quickly raise blood sugar levels and cause insulin spikes. **These blood sugar and insulin spikes are primary causes of weight gain.** These unhealthy carbs include candy, cakes, sweetened cereals, white rice, cookies, juice, soda, and white-flour products. With so many low-carb, heart-healthy, and whole-grain products in the marketplace today, there is no reason to be choosing refined foods.

On the Fat-Burning Food Plan, you will keep your refined sugar intake as low as possible. In fact, it's best if you avoid sugar altogether! This means steering clear of processed, high-glycemic carbs— since refined sugar has absolutely no nutritional value and will only detract you from the goals you are trying to achieve!

FATS

Most people think that fat makes you fat, but the truth is that it's really excess insulin production (caused by the overconsumption of sugar) that is mainly responsible for adding fat to your frame. Additionally, "fat-free" foods are often higher in sugar than their full-fat counterparts, which leads to more insulin production and eventually . . . more fat!

Try to eat healthy, heart-smart polyunsaturated or monosaturated fats (they don't clog the arteries). These types of fats are found in fish, olive oil, nuts, walnuts, avocados, and seeds. Avoid unhealthy fats such as saturated fats, hydrogenated fats, or trans fats found in chips, cakes, and fried foods.

FAT IS A CRITICAL PART OF OUR DIETS, SO DON'T SKIMP ON GOOD FATS. FAT IS NEEDED FOR THE FOLLOWING REASONS:

- It makes food taste good!
- It helps release a hormone to the brain called cholecystokinin (CCK), which tells the body, "I'm full. I'm satisfied. I can stop eating."
- It helps slow the entry rate of sugar (from carbohydrates) into the bloodstream, which gives you more long-term energy to last throughout your day!

WATER

Drink water! You need to stay hydrated! Water helps you absorb vitamins and minerals, flushes toxins out of the body, aids in digestion, keeps your skin healthy, and will help give you more energy and focus. Additionally, when you are dehydrated, you cannot efficiently burn fat! Aim for 6 to 8 eight-ounce glasses of pure water daily. It even curbs your appetite.

WHEN
TO EAT
WHAT
TO
DRINK

On the following pages, you will find the information needed to plan your daily menus for optimal fat-burning success.

WHEN
TO EAT

Lean lesson: Eat every 2 to 3 hours!

It's important to eat 5 times a day! Follow a regular eating schedule for a multitude of reasons. **First,** it keeps your blood sugar stable, instead of peaking and crashing (which can then lead to overeating). **Second,** eating frequently speeds up your metabolism by challenging it repeatedly. Timing is crucial to keep us on track—especially when it comes to eating! A "golden rule of eating": "Success follows those who eat often and early." Don't skip breakfast. Try not to eat late. See the sample eating schedule to the right.

WHAT
TO DRINK

Lean lesson: Drink calorie-free beverages!

- Drink 6 to 8 eight-ounce glasses of water a day.
- A glass of water 30 minutes before each meal will help curb your hunger.
- Avoid drinking with your meals. It may slow down your digestion. If you must, limit yourself to a small glass of water.
- Avoid all sugared soda.
- Diet soda and zero-calorie, artificially sweetened beverages are only OK in moderation, with a maximum of 1 per day.
- Coffee and tea are also fine in moderation, but avoid cream and sugar (if you need a sweetener, we suggest Stevia™, a natural root-based sweetener with no sugar or chemicals).
- Seltzer with lemon or lime.
- Herbal iced teas.
- Add lemon or lime to your water!

YOU SHOULD STRIVE TO EAT 5 TIMES A DAY, WHICH INCLUDES 3 MEALS AND 2 SNACKS. BELOW YOU WILL FIND A SAMPLE FOOD SCHEDULE TO FOLLOW.

SAMPLE EATING SCHEDULE

Breakfast:	7:00 AM
AM Snack:	9:30 AM
Lunch:	12:00 PM
Snack:	3:00 PM
Dinner:	6:00 PM

If those times don't work, create your own schedule. You might prefer to have a smaller portion for dinner and an evening snack around 8:00 PM. Always do what works best for you, but remember that your calories count! Even if you're eating healthy, if you're eating more calories than you need, you'll gain weight. Have a daily plan! Know what you'll be eating and when you'll be eating it! You're destined to be successful!

TOO BUSY TO EAT HEALTHY?

To achieve success, you must be prepared and have a plan that includes what and where you'll eat. Eat breakfast at home before you leave for work (so you're not tempted by coffee and donuts). Prepare your lunch for the next day the night before. Not only is brown bagging the healthier option, it's also a lot easier on your wallet! Shop for dinnertime groceries in bulk, which is an inexpensive way to get a lot of healthy food. You can just freeze what you are not using for the week!

A lot of us have busy lives: we go out to eat with friends; we watch our kids' basketball games that run late so we stop at a fast-food place before going home; we get tempted when we let ourselves go hungry for too long by working at our desks straight through lunch. So many of us are diverted or swayed from our goals because we haven't created a plan. By simply following the eating guidelines and the recipes in the Recipes for Life section, and carving out mealtimes, you are 90 percent there. Simply put, having a "plan of action" over the next few months will truly put you on the road to success.

RECIPES
FOR LIFE

With the Fat-Burning Food Guide, you are provided
with over **80 healthy gourmet breakfast, lunch, dinner,
and snack recipes!** This will be more than enough
to get you on your way and to help educate you
about how to prepare your meals. Use these recipes
to generate your own personal menu, mixing and
matching as you see fit.

PLEASE REMEMBER

The breakfast, lunch, and dinner meals will equal
approximately **1,000 calories per day.** To reach your
calorie requirements, you will need to add 2 or more
snacks each day to meet your calorie needs. Or
add 1 to 2 ounces of protein to your snack(s) and/or
meal(s). It's extremely important NOT to skip snacks
if you want to maintain your metabolism and preserve
muscle (because, "Muscle Burns Fat!").

BURN
BREAKFASTS

GOAT CHEESE AND TOMATO OMELET

2 WHOLE EGGS WHISKED WITH 1 TBSP. SKIM MILK
1 PLUM TOMATO, CHOPPED
1 OZ. CRUMBLED GOAT CHEESE
NONSTICK COOKING SPRAY

PREPARATION: Heat a nonstick skillet coated with nonstick cooking spray over medium heat. Add the whisked eggs and allow to cook for about 2 to 3 minutes. Then add in goat cheese and tomatoes and fold over into an omelet. Allow to cook for 1 to 2 additional minutes.

PUSH & LEAN PHASES: ADD 1 EGG WHITE AND ½ OZ. GOAT CHEESE.

VEGGIE SCRAMBLE

½ OF A GREEN ZUCCHINI, DICED
¼ OF A RED OR GREEN BELL PEPPER, DICED
3 TO 4 BROCCOLI FLORETS, CHOPPED
¼ CUP RED ONION, CHOPPED
1 LARGE WHOLE EGG WHISKED TOGETHER WITH 3 EGG WHITES
1 OZ. GRATED PARMESAN CHEESE
NONSTICK COOKING SPRAY

PREPARATION: Heat a nonstick skillet coated with nonstick cooking spray over medium heat. Add all vegetables and sauté for about 3 to 5 minutes, until they begin to soften. Add in egg mixture and scramble together; continue to cook until eggs are cooked through, about 3 to 4 minutes. Remove from heat and sprinkle with cheese.

PUSH & LEAN PHASES: ADD 1 WHOLE EGG.

EGG SANDWICH WITH CANADIAN BACON

Calories: 243
Protein: 23 g
Carbs: 12 g
Fiber: 2 g
Fat Total: 11 g

1 EGG WHISKED TOGETHER WITH 1 EGG WHITE
½ OZ. OF CANADIAN BACON
1 CUP STEAMED SPINACH LEAVES
2 TBSP. GRATED PARMESAN CHEESE
1 SLICE OF TOASTED
  LIGHT-STYLE WHOLE WHEAT BREAD
NONSTICK COOKING SPRAY*

*Please note that while nonstick cooking spray has fewer calories, there are 600 servings in a typical bottle. Use it sparingly!

PREPARATION: Heat a nonstick skillet coated with nonstick cooking spray over medium heat. Add the whisked eggs and scramble until cooked through, about 3 minutes. Then cook the Canadian bacon in the same pan until cooked through, about 4 to 5 minutes. Pile the eggs, bacon, and spinach on the toasted wheat bread and sprinkle with Parmesan cheese.

PUSH & LEAN PHASES: ADD 1 EGG WHITE, ½ OZ. OF CANADIAN BACON, AND 1 TBSP. OF PARMESAN CHEESE.

Calories: 242
Protein: 26 g
Carbs: 11 g
Fiber: 4 g
Fat Total: 10.5 g

Calories: 290
Protein: 26 g
Carbs: 22 g
Fiber: 4 g
Fat Total: 12 g

MOZZARELLA, SPINACH, AND TOMATO OMELET

3 EGG WHITES WHISKED WITH 1 TBSP. WATER
1 CUP FRESH SPINACH LEAVES
1 CUP DICED PLUM TOMATOES
¼ CUP PART-SKIM SHREDDED MOZZARELLA CHEESE
½ OF A WHOLE WHEAT LIGHT ENGLISH MUFFIN, TOASTED
NONSTICK COOKING SPRAY

PREPARATION: Heat a nonstick skillet coated with nonstick cooking spray over medium heat. Add the whisked eggs and allow to cook for about 2 to 3 minutes. Then add in spinach, tomatoes, and cheese and fold over into an omelet. Allow to cook for 2 to 3 additional minutes. Serve with toasted English muffin half.

PUSH & LEAN PHASES: ADD 1 EGG AND ½ LIGHT ENGLISH MUFFIN (SO YOU WILL NOW BE HAVING THE WHOLE MUFFIN).

CINNAMON RICOTTA CRUNCH

Calories: 201
Protein: 12 g
Carbs: 25 g
Fiber: 2.5 g
Fat Total: 6 g

1 CUP SKIM RICOTTA CHEESE
1 TSP. GROUND CINNAMON
2 TBSP. SLIVERED ALMONDS
½ CUP BERRIES

PREPARATION: Scoop the ricotta cheese into a cereal bowl. Mix in the cinnamon and berries. Top with slivered almonds.

PUSH & LEAN PHASES: ADD 1 TBSP. SLIVERED ALMONDS AND ¼ CUP BERRIES.

YOGURT WHEY SMOOTHIE

¾ CUP PLAIN NONFAT YOGURT

½ CUP FROZEN BERRIES

1 SCOOP OF WHEY PROTEIN POWDER*

ICE, TO TASTE

Calories: 258
Protein: 35 g
Carbs: 29 g
Fiber: 5 g
Fat Total: 2.5 g

PREPARATION: Add all ingredients in a blender, and blend until smooth and frothy.
*Beachbody® has a great Whey Protein Powder. Contact your Coach, or visit **Beachbody.com** or **TeamBeachbody.com** to order.

PUSH & LEAN PHASES: ADD ½ CUP BERRIES, ¼ CUP YOGURT, AND ½ SCOOP PROTEIN POWDER.

FONTINA OMELET

1 LARGE EGG WHISKED TOGETHER WITH 2 EGG WHITES

1 OZ. CHIVES, CHOPPED

1 OZ. FONTINA CHEESE, SLICED THIN

GRAPEFRUIT SEGMENTS FROM ONE PINK GRAPEFRUIT

NONSTICK COOKING SPRAY

Calories: 246
Protein: 20 g
Carbs: 12 g
Fiber: 1.5 g
Fat Total: 13 g

PREPARATION: Add the chopped chives to the whisked eggs and mix well. Heat a nonstick skillet coated with nonstick cooking spray over medium heat. Add eggs to the pan, but do not stir. Allow to set for 2 to 3 minutes; then add the cheese and fold over into an omelet. Cook for an additional 2 minutes. Serve with grapefruit segments.

PUSH & LEAN PHASES: ADD 1 WHOLE EGG.

BREAKFAST CAPRESE WITH PESTO SAUCE

1 WHOLE EGG WHISKED TOGETHER WITH 1 EGG WHITE

1 OZ. BUFFALO MOZZARELLA

2 SLICES TOMATO, RAW

½ CUP SLICED BUTTON MUSHROOMS

¼ OF A CHOPPED RED ONION

1 TBSP. PREPARED PESTO, ON THE SIDE

NONSTICK COOKING SPRAY

Calories: 272
Protein: 21 g
Carbs: 7 g
Fiber: 1 g
Fat Total: 18 g

PREPARATION: Heat a nonstick skillet coated with nonstick cooking spray over medium heat. Add mushrooms and onions and cook for 3 to 4 minutes. Add eggs and cook until firm—will set as an "open omelet." Remove eggs from pan, and top with slices of tomato and mozzarella and drizzle with pesto.

PUSH & LEAN PHASES: ADD 1 SLICE OF WHEAT TOAST.

EGG SALAD WRAP

1 LARGE HARD-BOILED EGG PLUS 2 HARD-BOILED EGG WHITES
½ TBSP. MAYONNAISE
¼ CUP FINELY DICED CELERY
2 ROMAINE LETTUCE LEAVES
1 6-IN. WHOLE WHEAT LOW-CARB TORTILLA
(ABOUT 60 CALORIES)
GROUND BLACK PEPPER
SALT
TABASCO SAUCE, IF DESIRED

Calories: 227
Protein: 16.5 g
Carbs: 22 g
Fiber: 2.5 g
Fat Total: 10.5 g

PREPARATION: Mix the eggs, mayonnaise, and celery in a bowl until well-combined. Season the eggs with salt and pepper to taste, and add a dash of Tabasco if desired. Pile mixture onto the tortilla and top with lettuce leaves. Roll up and enjoy.

PUSH & LEAN PHASES: ADD 1 NAVEL ORANGE.

HIGH-PROTEIN BREAKFAST WRAP

2 OZ. OF COOKED CHICKEN OR TURKEY BREAST, DICED
3 EGG WHITES, WHISKED
1 CUP OF SPINACH LEAVES
1 SLICE OF REDUCED-FAT SWISS CHEESE
1 6-IN. WHOLE WHEAT TORTILLA
(ABOUT 60 CALORIES)
NONSTICK COOKING SPRAY

Calories: 246
Protein: 32 g
Carbs: 21 g
Fiber: 2 g
Fat Total: 5.5 g

PREPARATION: Heat a nonstick skillet coated with nonstick cooking spray over medium heat. Add the chicken or turkey, eggs, and spinach and scramble. Cook until eggs are cooked through—about 5 minutes. Add the cheese and remove from heat. Pile mixture onto tortilla and wrap it up, and enjoy.

PUSH & LEAN PHASES: ADD 1 TO 2 OZ. OF CHICKEN OR TURKEY.

PEANUT BUTTER SMOOTHIE

1 CUP OF SKIM MILK OR SOY MILK

1 TBSP. PEANUT BUTTER

1 SCOOP OF WHEY VANILLA OR
WHEY CHOCOLATE PROTEIN POWDER*

ICE, TO TASTE

1 PACKET OF SPLENDA OR STEVIA, IF DESIRED

PREPARATION: Add all ingredients into a blender
and blend until smooth and frothy.

*Beachbody® has a great Whey Protein Powder. Contact your Coach, or visit
Beachbody.com or **TeamBeachbody.com** to order.

PUSH & LEAN PHASES: ADD ½ TBSP. PEANUT BUTTER.

SUNRISE QUESADILLA

1 6-IN. WHOLE WHEAT LOW-CARB TORTILLA,
CUT IN HALF (ABOUT 60 CALORIES WHOLE)

2 OZ. CHICKEN SAUSAGE, CRUMBLED

½ OZ. FONTINA CHEESE, SLICED THIN

½ CUP OF SLICED MUSHROOMS

¼ CUP SALSA (WITH ABOUT 10 TO 20
CALORIES PER 2 TBSP.)

SALT AND BLACK PEPPER TO TASTE

PREPARATION: Heat a nonstick
skillet over medium heat and add the
chicken sausage and mushrooms. Cook
until sausage is cooked through—about
5 to 8 minutes. Pile the sausage and
mushrooms on ½ of the tortilla and top
with the cheese; cover with other half of
the tortilla. Microwave quesadilla for
20 to 30 seconds and serve with salsa.

PUSH & LEAN PHASES: ADD 1 CUP OF MELON BALLS.

COTTAGE
CHEESE PARFAIT

¾ CUP OF 1%-MILK-FAT COTTAGE CHEESE
½ CUP OF FROZEN (THAWED) OR FRESH STRAWBERRIES
2 TBSP. CHOPPED WALNUTS

PREPARATION: Scoop the cottage cheese
into a cup, top with thawed strawberries, and
sprinkle walnuts over top.

Calories: 235
Protein: 25 g
Carbs: 13 g
Fiber: 2 g
Fat Total: 11 g

PUSH & LEAN PHASES: ADD 1 TBSP. OF WALNUTS
AND ½ CUP BERRIES.

OPEN-FACED BREAKFAST QUESADILLA WITH CHICKEN

3 OZ. GRILLED CHICKEN BREAST,
   CUT INTO STRIPS AND SEASONED WITH TACO SEASONING
1 6-IN. WHOLE WHEAT TORTILLA (ABOUT 60 CALORIES)
½ OZ. REDUCED-FAT SHREDDED CHEESE,
   ANY CHEESE OF YOUR CHOICE
1/3 CUP SPINACH LEAVES
1/3 CUP CHOPPED TOMATO
¼ CUP STORE-BOUGHT SALSA

> Calories: 255
> Protein: 27 g
> Carbs: 35 g
> Fiber: 4 g
> Fat Total: 4 g

PREPARATION: Lay the tortilla open-faced on a dinner plate. Top with chicken, cheese, spinach, and tomatoes. Microwave for 45 seconds and enjoy with salsa on the side.

PUSH & LEAN PHASES: ADD 1 TO 2 OZ. OF CHICKEN.

SCRAMBLED EGGS WITH GOAT CHEESE

1 LARGE EGG WHISKED TOGETHER WITH
   3 EGG WHITES AND 1 TBSP. WATER
1 OZ. GOAT CHEESE, CRUMBLED
2 TBSP. CHOPPED FRESH DILL,
   OR ½ TBSP. OF DRIED DILL
1 SLICE OF LIGHT-STYLE WHEAT TOAST
½ OF A SLICED BEEFSTEAK TOMATO
SALT AND PEPPER TO TASTE
NONSTICK COOKING SPRAY

> Calories: 267
> Protein: 25 g
> Carbs: 16.5 g
> Fiber: 2 g
> Fat Total: 11.5 g

PREPARATION: Spray a nonstick skillet with nonstick cooking spray, heat skillet over medium heat, and add the eggs. Cook for 2 to 3 minutes. Then add the cheese and dill and scramble until eggs are cooked through, about 1 to 2 additional minutes. Season with salt and pepper to taste and serve with toast and sliced tomatoes.

PUSH & LEAN PHASES: ADD 1 CUP OF MIXED BERRIES.

PUSH
BREAKFASTS

Enjoy one NEW Push Breakfast each week in the Push and Lean Phases.

PEANUT BUTTER TOAST

Calories: 254
Protein: 21 g
Carbs: 22 g
Fiber: 3 g
Fat Total: 10 g

1 SLICE OF WHEAT BREAD, TOASTED
1 TBSP. PEANUT BUTTER
1 TSP. LOW-SUGAR JAM
½ CUP 1%-MILK-FAT COTTAGE CHEESE

PREPARATION: Top toast with peanut butter and jam and serve with cottage cheese on the side.

HIGH-PROTEIN CEREAL BOWL

Calories: 285
Protein: 22 g
Carbs: 48 g
Fiber: 12 g
Fat Total: 5.5 g

1 CUP OF HIGH-FIBER, HIGH-PROTEIN CEREAL, SUCH AS KASHI GOLEAN
¾ CUP NONFAT MILK OR SOY MILK
½ CUP FRESH OR FROZEN RASPBERRIES
1 TBSP. CHOPPED WALNUTS

PREPARATION: Add all ingredients into a cereal bowl and enjoy!

BLUEBERRY-ALMOND OATMEAL

Calories: 273
Protein: 10.5 g
Carbs: 40 g
Fiber: 6 g
Fat Total: 8 g

1 CUP OF COOKED OATMEAL, MEASURED AFTER COOKING, COOKED WITH WATER
½ CUP FRESH OR FROZEN BLUEBERRIES
2 TBSP. SLIVERED ALMONDS
3 TBSP. SKIM OR SOY MILK
CINNAMON, IF DESIRED

PREPARATION: Prepare oats in a cereal bowl; stir in berries, almonds, and milk. Sprinkle with cinnamon, if desired.

LEAN
BREAKFASTS

Enjoy one NEW Lean Breakfast each week in the Lean Phase.

HOME-STYLE FRUIT-TOPPED WAFFLES

2 WHOLE WHEAT WAFFLES, IF POSSIBLE,
  LOOK FOR HIGHER-PROTEIN WAFFLES,
  SUCH AS KASHI GOLEAN
1 CUP OF FROZEN BERRIES, THAWED
1/3 CUP VANILLA YOGURT
1 TBSP. CHOPPED WALNUTS OR FLAXSEEDS
1 TBSP. GRADE B LOW-SUGAR MAPLE SYRUP, OPTIONAL

PREPARATION: Heat waffles in toaster oven and top with thawed berries, vanilla yogurt, and chopped nuts. Add low-sugar maple syrup if desired.

BAGEL BREAKFAST SANDWICH

1 WHOLE WHEAT BAGEL, SCOOP OUT SOME OF THE FLESH
FROM THE INNARDS OF THE BAGEL
3 OZ. OF NOVA SCOTIA SMOKED SALMON (LOX)*
2 TBSP. OF WHIPPED CREAM CHEESE
SLICED TOMATO AND SLICED RED ONION
1 CUP OF SLICED MELON AND BERRIES

PREPARATION: Toast bagel and spread cream cheese on top of both halves. Top with salmon, tomato, and onion and enjoy. Serve with melon and berries.

*Option: If you do not like Nova Scotia salmon, you can fill your bagel with scrambled eggs and 1 oz. of cheese.

HIGH-FIBER BREAKFAST MUFFIN

1-½ CUPS WHEAT BRAN FIBER
1 CUP LOW-FAT BUTTERMILK
1/3 CUP CANOLA OIL
1 EGG
2/3 CUP BROWN SUGAR, UNPACKED
½ TSP. VANILLA EXTRACT
1 CUP ALL-PURPOSE FLOUR
1 TSP. BAKING SODA
1 TSP. BAKING POWDER
½ TSP. SALT
½ CUP CHOPPED WALNUTS
12 PAPER MUFFIN LINERS

PREPARATION: Preheat oven to 375 degrees. Line 12 muffin cups with paper muffin liners. Mix the wheat bran and the buttermilk and allow to stand for 10 minutes. Then beat the oil, egg, sugar, and vanilla and add this to the bran mixture. In a separate bowl, mix the flour, baking soda, baking powder, and salt. Sift the flour mixture into the buttermilk mixture and combine, but do not overmix. Then fold in the walnuts. Spoon batter into muffin tins and bake for 15 to 20 minutes, or until a toothpick inserted in a muffin comes out clean.

Serve 1 muffin with ½ cup of cottage cheese or 1 egg for breakfast.

BURN

LUNCHES

SOUTHWEST SHRIMP SALAD

2 CUPS CLEANED, TORN ROMAINE LETTUCE LEAVES
5 OZ. SHRIMP, TAIL REMOVED AND SEASONED WITH
   OLD BAY SEASONING OR CAJUN SEASONING
1/3 CUP FROZEN CORN KERNELS, THAWED
5 CHERRY TOMATOES, HALVED
¼ OF A RED ONION, THINLY SLICED
2 TBSP. LOW-FAT ORGANIC OR ALL-NATURAL
   RANCH DRESSING
3 BAKED TORTILLA CHIPS, CRUSHED
NONSTICK COOKING SPRAY

Calories: 398
Protein: 33 g
Carbs: 35 g
Fiber: 6 g
Fat Total: 14 g

POACHED SALMON NIÇOISE

4-OZ. SALMON FILET
1 TBSP. BLACK PEPPERCORNS
3 CUPS DARK-GREEN LETTUCE LEAVES
1 BOILED RED NEW POTATO,
   CUT INTO QUARTERS
1 CUP OF STEAMED GREEN BEANS
1 PLUM TOMATO, QUARTERED
4 BLACK OLIVES
1 TBSP. LIGHT VINAIGRETTE DRESSING*

*Make sure dressing has no or low sugar content.

PREPARATION: In a large pot, add the peppercorns to 5 cups of water and bring to a rapid boil, then add the salmon and turn off the heat. Allow salmon to "poach" for 5 to 7 minutes, until cooked through. Remove salmon from water and allow it to cool. Meanwhile, pile greens onto a dinner plate and top with potato, green beans, tomato, and olives. Lay salmon on top of the salad and dress with salad dressing.

PUSH & LEAN PHASES: ADD 1 TO 2 OZ. OF SALMON.

Calories: 405
Protein: 41 g
Carbs: 32 g
Fiber: 6 g
Fat Total: 11.5 g

PREPARATION: Heat a nonstick skillet coated with nonstick cooking spray over medium heat. Add the shrimp and cook for 3 minutes on each side, until pink and cooked through. Meanwhile, pile the lettuce leaves on a dinner plate and top with the corn, tomatoes, red onion, and ranch dressing. Lastly, layer the shrimp on top of the salad and sprinkle with the crumbled tortilla chips.

PUSH & LEAN PHASES: ADD 1 TO 2 OZ. OF SHRIMP.

TUNA SALAD ON A BED

1 6-OZ. CAN OF TUNA PACKED IN WATER
2 TBSP. REDUCED-FAT NATURAL MAYONNAISE
¼ CUP DICED CELERY
DASH OF LEMON JUICE
3 CUPS OF MIXED DARK GREENS
½ OF A BEEFSTEAK TOMATO, SLICED
SALT AND PEPPER TO TASTE

PREPARATION: Make tuna salad by combining the tuna, mayonnaise, celery, and lemon juice; season with salt and pepper to taste. Pile greens onto a plate and top with tomato slices and tuna salad.

Calories: 370
Protein: 45 g
Carbs: 14 g
Fiber: 4.5 g
Fat Total: 15 g

PUSH & LEAN PHASES: ADD 2 TBSP. VINAIGRETTE DRESSING.

CHICKEN CAESAR SALAD

3 CUPS CLEAN, TORN ROMAINE
    LETTUCE LEAVES
4 OZ. OF PRECOOKED CHICKEN BREAST
3 TBSP. GRATED PARMESAN CHEESE
5 WHOLE-GRAIN CROUTONS (ABOUT
    50 TO 60 CALORIES FOR 5)
2 TBSP. REDUCED-CALORIE ORGANIC OR ALL-
    NATURAL CAESAR DRESSING OR 1 TBSP.
    OLIVE OIL MIXED WITH 2 TBSP. LEMON JUICE
SALT AND PEPPER TO TASTE

> Calories: 392
> Protein: 46 g
> Carbs: 11 g
> Fiber: 4 g
> Fat Total: 17 g

PREPARATION: On a large salad plate, pile the
lettuce and top with chicken and croutons. Sprinkle
the cheese over top and dress with either Caesar
dressing or lemon and olive oil; season to taste with
salt and pepper.

PUSH & LEAN PHASES: ADD 1 TO 2 OZ. OF CHICKEN.

TARRAGON CHICKEN SALAD PLATTER

4 OZ. OF POACHED WHITE-MEAT CHICKEN,
    CUT INTO ½-IN. CUBES
2 TBSP. LIGHT MAYONNAISE
½ TSP. DRIED TARRAGON
½ TSP. SEA SALT
½ TSP. PEPPER
½ OF A GRANNY SMITH APPLE, DICED
3 CUPS OF FRESH SPINACH LEAVES,
    WASHED AND TORN
3 WHOLE WHEAT MELBA TOASTS

> Calories: 400
> Protein: 42 g
> Carbs: 28 g
> Fiber: 4 g
> Fat Total: 15 g

PREPARATION: Combine chicken with mayonnaise,
tarragon, salt, and apple; mix well and season with
fresh pepper. Pile on top of fresh spinach leaves and
serve with melba toast.

PUSH & LEAN PHASES: ADD 1 TO 2 OZ. OF CHICKEN.

Calories: 398
Protein: 30 g
Carbs: 43 g
Fiber: 7 g
Fat Total: 10 g

ASIAN-STYLE STIR-FRY

4-OZ. FILET MIGNON

1/3 OF A RED BELL PEPPER, DICED

4 BROCCOLI FLORETS

¼ OF A MEDIUM ONION, DICED

½ CUP SNOW PEAS

¼ CUP SLICED SHIITAKE MUSHROOMS

1 TSP. REDUCED-SODIUM SOY SAUCE

1 TBSP. ORANGE JUICE

½ TSP. GINGER, MINCED

1 TSP. SESAME SEEDS

1 TSP. CORNSTARCH MIXED WITH 1/3 CUP WATER

½ CUP BROWN RICE, MEASURED AFTER COOKING

SALT AND PEPPER TO TASTE

PREPARATION: Make stir-fry sauce by combining the soy sauce, orange juice, ginger, sesame seeds, and water/cornstarch mixture. Clean and cut filet into slices, season with salt and pepper, and sauté in a nonstick skillet over medium heat for 1 to 2 minutes. Then add all other vegetables and the stir-fry sauce. Cook over medium heat for about 8 to 10 minutes, until the vegetables begin to soften. Serve over brown rice.

PUSH & LEAN PHASES: ADD 1 TO 2 OZ. OF FILET MIGNON.

CHICKEN PICCATA WITH STEAMED ASPARAGUS

4-OZ. BONELESS, SKINLESS CHICKEN BREAST, BUTTERFLIED
¼ CUP WHITE WINE
¼ CUP FRESH LEMON JUICE
2 TSP. OLIVE OIL
1 TSP. CAPERS
12 ASPARAGUS SPEARS, STEAMED
MRS. DASH ITALIAN SEASONING TO TASTE
SALT AND PEPPER TO TASTE

PREPARATION: Season chicken breast with Mrs. Dash. Heat a nonstick skillet over medium heat and add olive oil. Cook chicken breast for about 2 to 3 minutes on each side, until golden brown. Then add white wine, lemon juice, and capers and simmer until chicken is cooked through. Season with salt and pepper to taste and serve with asparagus spears.

PUSH & LEAN PHASES: ADD 1 TO 2 OZ. OF CHICKEN.

VEGGIE BURGER

2 PROTEIN-BASED VEGGIE BURGERS (ABOUT 90 CALORIES EACH)
1 WHOLE WHEAT LIGHT-STYLE ENGLISH MUFFIN, TOASTED
2 SLICES OF A BEEFSTEAK TOMATO
2 1-IN. SLICES OF AVOCADO
1 CUP ROMAINE LETTUCE
½ OF A SLICED CUCUMBER
2 HEARTS OF PALM, SLICED INTO ROUNDS
FRESH LEMON JUICE

Calories: 395
Protein: 20 g
Carbs: 58 g
Fiber: 15 g
Fat Total: 12 g

PREPARATION: Cook veggie burgers according to package directions and pile onto half of the English muffin; then top with tomato and avocado and the other half of the English muffin. Make a side salad by combining lettuce, cucumber, hearts of palm, and fresh lemon juice.

PUSH & LEAN PHASES: ADD 1 SLICE OF LOW-FAT CHEESE ON THE VEGGIE BURGER.

SOUTHWEST TURKEY BURGER

4 OZ. OF LEAN, WHITE-MEAT TURKEY, GROUND
4 TBSP. OF COMMERCIALLY PREPARED SALSA
¼ CUP FROZEN CORN KERNEL, DEFROSTED
2 1-IN. SLICES OF AVOCADO
1 SLICE OF TOMATO
1 WHOLE WHEAT LIGHT-STYLE ENGLISH MUFFIN,
  OR A WHOLE-GRAIN HAMBURGER BUN OR PITA
MIXED GREENS, SUCH AS ARUGULA,
  ROMAINE, AND SPINACH
1 TSP. LEMON JUICE

Calories: 406
Protein: 29 g
Carbs: 30 g
Fiber: 6.5 g
Fat Total: 19 g

PREPARATION: Combine turkey meat, salsa, and corn kernels— form into a patty and grill or broil for about 5 minutes on each side, until cooked through. Make a sandwich with the turkey burger, tomato, and avocado on the English muffin. Top the mixed greens with fresh lemon juice.

PUSH & LEAN PHASES: ADD 1 TO 2 OZ. OF TURKEY.

CHICKEN QUESADILLA

Calories: 396
Protein: 50 g
Carbs: 31 g
Fiber: 4.5 g
Fat Total: 10 g

4-OZ. BONELESS, SKINLESS CHICKEN BREAST

1 6-IN. WHOLE WHEAT LOW-CARB TORTILLA (ABOUT 60 CALORIES)

½ CUP DICED TOMATO

2 ROMAINE LETTUCE LEAVES, SHREDDED

¼ CUP REDUCED-FAT CHEDDAR CHEESE, SHREDDED

¼ CUP SALSA

TACO SEASONING TO TASTE

CILANTRO TO TASTE

PREPARATION: Season chicken with taco seasoning and grill or broil on both sides until cooked through. Cut chicken into strips and pile the chicken, tomatoes, lettuce, cheese, and salsa onto tortilla and wrap. Garnish with fresh cilantro, if desired.

PUSH & LEAN PHASES: ADD 1 TO 2 OZ. OF CHICKEN.

SASHIMI AND SALAD

Calories: 396
Protein: 36.5 g
Carbs: 14 g
Fiber: 5 g
Fat Total: 22 g

2 OZ. RAW TUNA, SLICED
2 OZ. RAW SALMON, SLICED
½ CUP STEAMED EDAMAME
1 CUP OF SALAD GREENS TOPPED WITH 1 TBSP. GINGER SESAME DRESSING
1 TBSP. REDUCED-SODIUM SOY SAUCE
GINGER AND WASABI TO SEASON AND TO TASTE

PREPARATION: Order lunch as specified above.

PUSH & LEAN STAGES: ADD 1 TO 2 OZ. OF SALMON OR TUNA.

CAJUN FISH TACOS

Calories: 388
Protein: 50 g
Carbs: 24 g
Fiber: 8 g
Fat Total: 11 g

5-OZ. FISH FILET, WHITE FLAKY FISH
4 LEAVES BUTTERLEAF LETTUCE
½ CUP CABBAGE, SHREDDED
¼ CUP REDUCED-FAT CHEDDAR CHEESE, SHREDDED
1 PLUM TOMATO, DICED
1/3 CUP CANNED BLACK BEANS, RINSED OF BRINE
¼ CUP STORE-BOUGHT SALSA
CAJUN SEASONING

PREPARATION: Preheat oven to 300 degrees. Coat fish with Cajun seasoning, place onto a baking pan, and bake for 12 to 18 minutes or until done. Drain excess juice and transfer to clean plate before cooling. Wrap fish in lettuce leaves with cabbage, cheese, and tomatoes. Serve with side of black beans and salsa.

PUSH & LEAN PHASES: ADD 1 TO 2 OZ. OF FISH.

GRILLED SALMON BURGER

5-OZ. SALMON FILET, FINELY DICED
1 CELERY STALK, DICED
¼ OF A RED ONION, DICED
1 TSP. FRESH DILL, CHOPPED
1 EGG WHITE, BEATEN
2 CUPS CLEANED, TORN ROMAINE
 OR SPINACH LETTUCE
3 1-IN. SLICES OF AVOCADO
SALT AND PEPPER TO TASTE
NONSTICK COOKING SPRAY

PREPARATION: Heat a nonstick skillet coated with nonstick cooking spray over medium heat. Then sauté the celery and the onions until translucent and allow to cool. In a bowl, combine the salmon, cooled celery/onions, dill, egg white, and salt and pepper and form into a patty. Grill or broil the patty for about 5 to 6 minutes on each side until cooked through. Serve over a bed of romaine or spinach and top with avocado slices.

PUSH & LEAN PHASES: ADD 1 TO 2 OZ. OF SALMON.

GREEK CHICKEN PITA

Calories: 407
Protein: 42 g
Carbs: 25 g
Fiber: 4 g
Fat Total: 15 g

1 CUP CLEANED, TORN ROMAINE LETTUCE LEAVES
4 OZ. OF GRILLED CHICKEN BREAST, CUT INTO STRIPS
½ OF A CUCUMBER, SLICED
2 TBSP. REDUCED-FAT CRUMBLED FETA CHEESE
3 BLACK OLIVES, SLICED
1 TBSP. LIGHT VINAIGRETTE
½ OF A 6-IN. WHOLE WHEAT PITA POCKET
½ OF A RED OR ORANGE PEPPER, CUT INTO SLICES

PREPARATION: In a bowl, combine the lettuce, chicken, cucumber, feta cheese, olives, and vinaigrette. Pile the salad mixture into the pita pocket and enjoy. Serve with fresh pepper slices.

PUSH & LEAN PHASES: ADD 1 TO 2 OZ. OF CHICKEN.

CHEF SALAD WITH RUSSIAN DRESSING

2 TO 3 CUPS DARK LETTUCE LEAVES
3-OZ. SLICED TURKEY BREAST,
   CUT INTO STRIPS
1 OZ. REDUCED-FAT SWISS CHEESE,
   CUT INTO STRIPS
5 BLACK OLIVES, HALVED
1 PLUM TOMATO, CHOPPED
1 TBSP. LIGHT MAYONNAISE
1 TBSP. KETCHUP
3 WHOLE WHEAT MELBA TOASTS

Calories: 371
Protein: 30.5 g
Carbs: 29 g
Fiber: 5 g
Fat Total: 17 g

PREPARATION: On a large dinner plate, pile the lettuce and top with turkey, cheese, olives, and tomato. In a separate bowl, make the Russian dressing by combining the ketchup and mayonnaise. Dress the salad and serve with Melba toasts.

PUSH & LEAN PHASES: ADD 1 TO 2 OZ. OF TURKEY.

PUSH
LUNCHES

Enjoy one NEW Push Lunch each week in the Push and Lean Phases.

OPEN-FACED TUNA MELT

1 SLICE WHOLE WHEAT TOAST
1 CAN OR 6 OZ. OF TUNA PACKED IN WATER
1 TBSP. LIGHT MAYONNAISE
1 SLICE OF REDUCED-FAT CHEESE
1 SLICE OF TOMATO

> **Calories: 415**
> **Protein: 52 g**
> **Carbs: 15 g**
> **Fiber: 2 g**
> **Fat Total: 15.5 g**

PREPARATION: Make the tuna salad by combining the tuna with the mayonnaise. Pile about half of the tuna salad on the wheat toast and top with the tomato and cheese. Bake in the toaster at 350 degrees for about 5 to 8 minutes, until the cheese melts. Enjoy the rest of the tuna salad in a bowl.

SUSHI PLATTER

LEAN LESSON: YOU CAN ASK FOR NEARLY ANY SUSHI ROLL AS A "CUT
  ROLL" WITHOUT RICE, ESPECIALLY IF BROWN RICE IS NOT OFFERED.

1 SPICY TUNA ROLL OR OTHER
  SUSHI ROLL MADE WITH BROWN RICE

2 PIECES OF SASHIMI OR SUSHI
  MADE WITH BROWN RICE

½ CUP STEAMED EDAMAME

GREEN SALAD TOPPED WITH 1 TBSP.
  GINGER SESAME SALAD DRESSING

PREPARATION: Order lunch as specified above.

LEAN
LUNCHES

Enjoy one NEW Lean Lunch each week in the Lean Phase.

OVERSTUFFED DELI SANDWICH

2 SLICES OF WHOLE-GRAIN BREAD
3 TO 4 OZ. OF DELI TURKEY
  OR LEAN ROAST BEEF
1 SLICE OF CHEESE OF CHOICE
SLICED TOMATO
1 TBSP. MAYONNAISE, LIGHT IF AVAILABLE
MUSTARD, IF DESIRED
SIDE SALAD WITH LIGHT VINAIGRETTE,
  IF DESIRED

Calories: 463
Protein: 42 g
Carbs: 38 g
Fiber: 5 g
Fat Total: 15.5 g

PIZZA

1 SLICE OF CHEESE PIZZA TOPPED WITH
  GRILLED CHICKEN OR SHRIMP
LARGE GARDEN SALAD DRESSED WITH
  2 TBSP. VINAIGRETTE DRESSING

PREPARATION: Order lunch as
specified above.

Calories: 475
Protein: 41 g
Carbs: 45 g
Fiber: 7 g
Fat Total: 15 g

PREPARATION: Order sandwich as specified above. Enjoy with a pickle, if desired.

BURN

DINNERS

TUNA OR SALMON SASHIMI

6-OZ. TUNA OR SALMON STEAK
2 TBSP. PONZU SAUCE
2 TBSP. SLICED GREEN ONIONS
MIXED GREEN SALAD
2 TBSP. ASIAN SESAME DRESSING
SALT AND PEPPER TO TASTE
NONSTICK COOKING SPRAY

Calories: 369
Protein: 35 g
Carbs: 9.5 g
Fiber: 1 g
Fat Total: 20 g

PREPARATION: Season the tuna or salmon with salt and pepper on all sides. Sear on all sides in a nonstick skillet coated with nonstick cooking spray, until sides turn opaque. Cut into thin slices. Mix the ponzu with green onions and pour over the tuna or salmon. Serve with salad.

PUSH & LEAN PHASES: ADD 1 TO 2 OZ. OF TUNA OR SALMON.

DIJON BAKED SEA BASS WITH PARMESAN CAULIFLOWER

5-OZ. SEA BASS
2 TBSP. LEMON JUICE
1 TBSP. DIJON MUSTARD
2 TSP. OLIVE OIL
2 TBSP. MINCED FRESH PARSLEY
   OR 1 TBSP. DRIED PARSLEY
1 CUP OF CAULIFLOWER FLORETS
2 TBSP. GRATED PARMESAN CHEESE
SEA SALT AND PEPPER TO TASTE
NONSTICK COOKING SPRAY

Calories: 361
Protein: 41.5 g
Carbs: 7.5 g
Fiber: 2 g
Fat Total: 18 g

PREPARATION: Preheat oven to 425 degrees. In a small bowl, combine the lemon juice, mustard, olive oil, and parsley. Place sea bass in an ovenproof dish and top with the lemon sauce. Place in the oven and bake for about 20 minutes or until fish flakes easily with a fork. Meanwhile, spray a baking sheet with nonstick cooking spray and lay cauliflower down in one layer; season with a pinch of sea salt and black pepper and top with Parmesan cheese. Bake at 425 degrees for 20 minutes. (Tip: Fish and cauliflower can bake in the oven together.)

PUSH & LEAN PHASES: ADD 1 TO 2 OZ. OF SEA BASS.

COUNTRY-STYLE PORK CHOPS WITH SAUTÉED SPINACH

5-OZ. CENTER-CUT LEAN, BONELESS
  PORK CHOP
1 TSP. LEMON PEPPER
2 TBSP. SHALLOTS, CHOPPED
1 TBSP. COUNTRY-STYLE MUSTARD
2 TBSP. CHICKEN BROTH
2 TBSP. WATER
2 CUPS FRESH SPINACH LEAVES
4 CHERRY TOMATOES, HALVED
2 TBSP. GRATED PARMESAN CHEESE
SALT TO TASTE
NONSTICK COOKING SPRAY

PREPARATION: Season pork chop with salt and lemon pepper, and sear in a nonstick skillet coated with nonstick cooking spray, for about 5 minutes on each side or until cooked through. Remove chop from pan. In the same pan, sauté the shallots for about 2 minutes. Then add mustard, chicken stock, and water and reduce until thick—should coat the back of a spoon. Top the pork chop with the sauce. In the same pan, sauté spinach and tomatoes until the spinach is wilted. Top spinach and tomatoes with grated Parmesan cheese.

PUSH & LEAN PHASES: ADD 1 TO 2 OZ. OF PORK.

CHICKEN KABOBS WITH OVEN-ROASTED ZUCCHINI

5-OZ. BONELESS, SKINLESS CHICKEN BREAST, CUT INTO 1-IN. CUBES

1 TSP. OLIVE OIL

2 TBSP. LEMON JUICE

¼ CUP RED ONIONS, THINLY SLICED

1 TSP. PAPRIKA

1 TSP. MRS. DASH

1 CUP OF BELL PEPPERS (RED, YELLOW, AND GREEN), CUT INTO 1-IN. CUBES

1 CUP GREEN ZUCCHINI, CUT INTO 1-½-IN. ROUNDS

SEA SALT TO TASTE

3 WOODEN OR METAL KABOB STICKS

NONSTICK COOKING SPRAY

PREPARATION: Marinate the chicken in the olive oil, lemon juice, red onions, and paprika for 30 minutes. Then season the chicken with Mrs. Dash; skewer chicken cubes with the bell peppers onto the kabob sticks. Grill or broil until cooked through, about 8 minutes. Meanwhile, arrange the zucchini slices onto a baking sheet, season with sea salt, and spray with nonstick cooking spray. Bake at 375 degrees for 12 to 15 minutes, or until soft.

PUSH & LEAN PHASES: ADD 1 TO 2 OZ. OF CHICKEN.

Calories: 364
Protein: 39 g
Carbs: 17 g
Fiber: 6 g
Fat Total: 16 g

CHERRY TOMATO SALMON

6-OZ. SALMON FILET
3 CHERRY TOMATOES, HALVED
2 TBSP. FRESH LEMON JUICE
1 TSP. LEMON PEPPER
½ TBSP. CHOPPED THYME
½ TBSP. CHOPPED ROSEMARY
2 CUPS KALE, CLEANED AND TORN
SEA SALT AND BLACK PEPPER TO TASTE
2 TSP. OLIVE OIL

PREPARATION: Place salmon filet in a baking dish, and season with lemon pepper, thyme, and fresh lemon juice. Top with cherry tomatoes. Bake at 325 degrees until done, about 20 minutes. Meanwhile, heat a nonstick skillet coated with olive oil over medium heat; add kale leaves and season with sea salt and pepper. Simmer until soft, about 8 to 10 minutes.

PUSH & LEAN PHASES: ADD 1 TO 2 OZ. OF SALMON.

BALSAMIC FLANK STEAK WITH SAUTÉED SPINACH AND FAUX MASHED POTATOES

4-OZ. FLANK STEAK

2 TBSP. BALSAMIC VINEGAR

2 TSP. OLIVE OIL

2 TSP. DRIED ROSEMARY, MINCED

1 CUP SPINACH LEAVES, WASHED

2 CUPS CAULIFLOWER FLORETS, STEAMED UNTIL SOFT

NONSTICK COOKING SPRAY

COWBOY STEAK WITH OVEN-ROASTED MUSHROOMS AND ONIONS

4-OZ. FILET MIGNON OR LEAN SIRLOIN

1 TSP. GROUND COFFEE

1 TSP. CAYENNE PEPPER

1 CUP OF SLICED BUTTON MUSHROOMS

½ OF A RED ONION, SLICED

1 TSP. OLIVE OIL

SALT AND PEPPER TO TASTE

NONSTICK COOKING SPRAY

Calories: 377
Protein: 37 g
Carbs: 20 g
Fiber: 4 g
Fat Total: 17 g

PREPARATION: Rub the steak with the coffee, cayenne pepper, and salt and pepper and grill or broil for about 3 minutes on each side, or until desired doneness. Meanwhile, spray a baking sheet with nonstick cooking spray and arrange the mushrooms and onions in a single layer and season with salt and pepper and drizzle with olive oil. Roast at 375 degrees for about 15 to 20 minutes.

PUSH & LEAN PHASES: ADD 1 TO 2 OZ. OF FILET MIGNON OR LEAN SIRLOIN.

Calories: 353
Protein: 30 g
Carbs: 17 g
Fiber: 7 g
Fat Total: 19.5 g

PREPARATION: In a zip-top bag, combine the vinegar, oil, and rosemary; add the flank steak into the bag and marinate for 30 to 60 minutes. Then cook steak on a grill or in a broiler for about 5 minutes on each side. Meanwhile, heat a nonstick skillet coated with nonstick cooking spray over medium heat, and add spinach leaves; season with salt and pepper and sauté for 3 to 5 minutes. Lastly, blend the steamed cauliflower florets in a blender or food processor until smooth and then heat in the microwave.

PUSH & LEAN PHASES: ADD 1 TO 2 OZ. OF FLANK STEAK.

LEMON-HERBED TILAPIA WITH GREEN BEANS PROVENCAL

6-OZ. TILAPIA FILET
JUICE OF 1 LEMON
½ TSP. DRIED THYME
½ TSP. DRIED ROSEMARY
3 TBSP. WHOLE WHEAT BREAD CRUMBS
1 TSP. OLIVE OIL
1 CUP GREEN BEANS, STEAMED
4 TBSP. MARINARA TOMATO SAUCE
SALT AND PEPPER TO TASTE

Calories: 383
Protein: 42 g
Carbs: 29 g
Fiber: 6 g
Fat Total: 10 g

PREPARATION: Preheat oven to 400 degrees. Spray an ovenproof dish with nonstick cooking spray and place tilapia filet in dish. Season the fish with salt and pepper. Then drizzle fish with olive oil and lemon, sprinkle with herbs, and dust with bread crumbs. Bake in the oven for 20 minutes or until fish flakes easily with a fork. Meanwhile, microwave the green beans and the tomato sauce for 1 minute, or until heated thoroughly.

PUSH & LEAN PHASES: ADD 1 TO 2 OZ. OF TILAPIA.

PONZU GRILLED SALMON WITH SAUTÉED BOK CHOY

Calories: 385
Protein: 36 g
Carbs: 14 g
Fiber: 2 g
Fat Total: 20 g

6-OZ. SALMON FILET
¼ CUP ORANGE JUICE
½ TSP. HONEY
1 TSP. REDUCED-SODIUM SOY SAUCE
1 TSP. WHITE WINE
1 TSP. LIME JUICE
¼ TSP. CRUSHED RED PEPPER
2 CUPS BOK CHOY, CLEANED AND ROUGHLY CUT
2 TSP. OLIVE OIL
SALT AND PEPPER TO TASTE

PREPARATION: Combine orange juice, honey, soy sauce, white wine, lime juice, and red pepper to make sauce. Season salmon with salt and pepper and brush with sauce (reserve some sauce to top finished salmon). Grill or broil the salmon until done, about 5 minutes on each side depending on the thickness of the filet. Meanwhile, heat a nonstick skillet over medium heat; add the olive oil and the bok choy. Sauté for about 6 to 7 minutes, or until soft, and season with salt and pepper. Top the salmon with the remaining sauce and serve with the bok choy.

PUSH & LEAN PHASES: ADD 1 TO 2 OZ. OF SALMON.

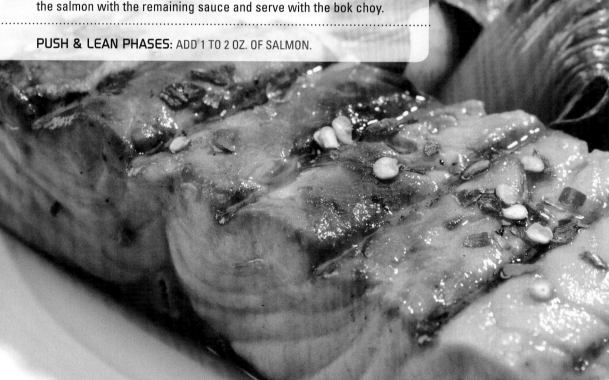

CHICKEN BRUSCHETTA

5-OZ. BONELESS, SKINLESS CHICKEN BREAST, BUTTERFLIED

1 TSP. ONION POWDER

1 TSP. CHILI POWDER

1 PLUM TOMATO, DICED

2 TBSP. FRESH BASIL, THINLY SLICED

1 TSP. GARLIC, MINCED

1 TSP. OLIVE OIL

2 CUPS STEAMED GREEN BEANS

SALT AND PEPPER TO TASTE

PREPARATION: Season chicken with onion powder and chili powder, and grill or broil until done, about 4 to 5 minutes per side. To make bruschetta, combine tomatoes, basil, and minced garlic and season with salt and pepper to taste. Top chicken with the bruschetta and serve with steamed green beans.

PUSH & LEAN PHASES: ADD 1 TO 2 OZ. OF CHICKEN.

STEAK FAJITAS

4-OZ. FLANK STEAK, CUT INTO STRIPS

½ OF A RED BELL PEPPER, CUT INTO STRIPS

½ OF A YELLOW BELL PEPPER, CUT INTO STRIPS

¼ OF A WHITE OR RED ONION, CUT INTO STRIPS

1 TSP. GARLIC POWDER

¼ TSP. CUMIN

¼ TSP. SALT

¼ TSP. PEPPER

¼ CUP SALSA

1 6-IN. WHOLE WHEAT LOW-CARB TORTILLA
  (ABOUT 60 CALORIES)

1 PLUM TOMATO, CUT INTO EIGHTHS

½ CUCUMBER, PEELED AND SLICED
  INTO ½-IN. ROUNDS

5 BLACK OLIVES, SLICED

JUICE OF 1 FRESH LIME

NONSTICK COOKING SPRAY

Calories: 365
Protein: 28 g
Carbs: 39 g
Fiber: 4.5 g
Fat Total: 14 g

PREPARATION: Heat a nonstick skillet coated with nonstick cooking spray over medium heat and add the steak. Sauté steak for about 2 minutes, allowing it to "brown," and season with salt, pepper, and cumin. Add peppers, onions, and garlic powder and sauté for an additional 3 to 4 minutes, until the steak is cooked through and the peppers have begun to soften. Serve with salsa and warmed tortilla. While fajitas are cooking, combine the cucumber, tomato, and olives and top with fresh lime juice and salt and pepper to taste.

PUSH & LEAN PHASES: ADD 1 TO 2 OZ. OF STEAK.

Calories: 363
Protein: 37 g
Carbs: 17.5 g
Fiber: 6 g
Fat Total: 17 g

GINGER LEMON PORK WITH OVEN-ROASTED BRUSSELS SPROUTS

5-OZ. PORK TENDERLOIN
3 TBSP. CHOPPED WHITE ONION
1 TSP. MINCED GARLIC
1 TBSP. OLIVE OIL
1 TBSP. REDUCED-SODIUM SOY SAUCE
1 TBSP. FRESH LEMON JUICE
½ TSP. GRATED LEMON ZEST, PEEL
1 TSP. MINCED GINGER
8 BRUSSELS SPROUTS, CLEANED AND TRIMMED
SEA SALT AND PEPPER TO TASTE
NONSTICK COOKING SPRAY

PREPARATION: Preheat oven to 375 degrees. Combine the onion, garlic, olive oil, soy sauce, lemon juice, lemon zest, and ginger in a zip-top bag and add the pork. Marinate the pork for 30 to 60 minutes. Remove pork from marinade, season with salt and pepper, and sear in an ovenproof nonstick skillet on all sides. Then place the pork, in the skillet, into the oven and bake until cooked through—about 15 to 20 minutes. Meanwhile, spray a baking sheet with nonstick cooking spray and place the sprouts on the sheet. Season with salt and pepper, and roast in the oven for 20 to 25 minutes.

PUSH & LEAN PHASES: ADD 1 TO 2 OZ. OF PORK.

SHRIMP AND CHICKEN STIR-FRY SERVED OVER ASIAN GREENS

2-OZ. CHICKEN BREAST, CUT INTO STRIPS

3 TO 4 LARGE SHRIMP, WHOLE, CLEANED, AND TAIL REMOVED

¼ CUP WATER CHESTNUTS, SLICED

2 TBSP. SLIVERED ALMONDS

2 TBSP. GREEN ONIONS, SLICED

1 TBSP. MINCED GINGER ROOT

1 TBSP. MINCED GARLIC

2 TBSP. LIME JUICE

2 TBSP. ORANGE JUICE

1 TSP. REDUCED-SODIUM SOY SAUCE

2 CUPS WATERCRESS, REMOVE BOTTOM 2 IN.

1 CUP SPINACH, CLEANED LEAVES

½ CUP BEAN SPROUTS

2 TSP. SESAME OIL

NONSTICK COOKING SPRAY

PREPARATION: Heat a nonstick skillet coated with nonstick cooking spray over medium heat. Add the green onions, garlic, and ginger and sauté for 1 minute. Then add the shrimp and chicken and stir-fry for about 3 to 4 minutes, until the chicken and shrimp are almost done. Then add the lime juice, orange juice, soy sauce, almonds, and water chestnuts and bring to a simmer. Cook for an additional 2 minutes or until chicken and shrimp are fully cooked. Remove mixture from pan, and add sesame oil to pan and heat over medium-high heat; add the watercress, spinach, and bean sprouts and sauté for 4 to 5 minutes. Serve the stir-fry over the Asian greens.

PUSH & LEAN PHASES: ADD 1 TO 2 OZ. OF CHICKEN OR SHRIMP.

Calories: 370
Protein: 37 g
Carbs: 17 g
Fiber: 5 g
Fat Total: 18 g

CHICKEN MARSALA WITH BRAISED BROCCOLI

5-OZ. BONELESS, SKINLESS CHICKEN BREAST, BUTTERFLIED
1 TSP. MRS. DASH ITALIAN SEASONING
2 TBSP. CHOPPED ONION
½ CUP SLICED BUTTON MUSHROOMS
3 TBSP. MARSALA WINE
1 TSP. OLIVE OIL
1 TSP. DRIED ROSEMARY
1 CUP BROCCOLI FLORETS
NONSTICK COOKING SPRAY

Calories: 354
Protein: 36 g
Carbs: 23 g
Fiber: 3 g
Fat Total: 9 g

PREPARATION: Season butterflied chicken breast with Mrs. Dash Italian seasoning. Heat a nonstick skillet sprayed with nonstick cooking spray over medium heat. Sauté chicken breast until cooked through and golden brown on each side—about 3 to 4 minutes per side. Remove chicken from pan and add olive oil, onion, mushrooms, and rosemary; sauté on medium-low heat for 3 to 4 minutes, until mushrooms begin to give off fluid. Add the marsala wine and simmer for 2 to 3 minutes, until reduced by half. Top chicken with the marsala wine sauce. Meanwhile, steam the broccoli in the microwave for about 3 to 4 minutes, or until desired degree of softness.

PUSH & LEAN PHASES: ADD 1 TO 2 OZ. OF CHICKEN.

HALIBUT WITH BLACK-BEAN RELISH

6-OZ. HALIBUT FILET OR STEAK
1 TSP. CHOPPED FRESH ROSEMARY, OR ½ TSP. DRIED
1 TSP. CHOPPED FRESH DILL, OR ½ TSP. DRIED
1 TSP. CHOPPED FRESH PARSLEY, OR ½ TSP. DRIED
SALT AND PEPPER

FOR SAUCE

¼ CUP BLACK BEANS
2 TBSP. RED ONIONS, MINCED
2 TBSP. TOMATO, DICED
2 TBSP. LEMON JUICE
1 TBSP. MINCED CILANTRO
1 TSP. DRIED CUMIN
SALT AND PEPPER TO TASTE

FOR GREEK SALAD

2 CUPS TORN ROMAINE LETTUCE LEAVES
½ OF A SLICED CUCUMBER
2 TBSP. REDUCED-FAT CRUMBLED FETA CHEESE
3 CHERRY TOMATOES, HALVED
2 TBSP. FRESH LEMON JUICE

Calories: 381
Protein: 54 g
Carbs: 19 g
Fiber: 6 g
Fat Total: 10 g

PREPARATION: Season halibut with herbs and salt and pepper and grill or broil until cooked through—about 5 minutes on each side, more or less, depending on the thickness of the fish. Meanwhile, combine all ingredients for the relish. For Greek salad, toss the ingredients together in a salad bowl. Top the fish with the black-bean sauce and enjoy the salad on the side.

PUSH & LEAN PHASES: ADD 1 TO 2 OZ. OF HALIBUT.

PUSH
DINNERS

Enjoy one NEW Push Dinner each week in
the Push and Lean Phases.

CHICKEN PARMESAN WITH ITALIAN GREENS

5-OZ. BONELESS, SKINLESS CHICKEN BREAST
1 EGG WHITE, WHISKED
¼ CUP WHOLE WHEAT BREAD CRUMBS
1/3 CUP SHREDDED PART-SKIM MOZZARELLA CHEESE
½ CUP CANNED TOMATO SAUCE
2 TBSP. GRATED PARMESAN CHEESE
1 CUP BROCCOLI RABE (RAPINI) OR ESCAROLE,
 CLEANED AND ROUGHLY CHOPPED
1 CLOVE OF GARLIC, MINCED
SALT AND PEPPER TO TASTE
NONSTICK COOKING SPRAY

PREPARATION: Preheat oven to 375 degrees. Dip
the chicken breast in egg white and coat with the
bread crumbs. In an ovenproof baking dish, bake the
chicken for about 15 minutes, until cooked almost all
the way through. Pull chicken out of the oven and
top with the tomato sauce, mozzarella cheese, and
Parmesan cheese. Bake again for about 15 minutes,
until cheese melts and chicken is cooked through.
Meanwhile, heat a nonstick skillet coated with
nonstick cooking spray. Add the garlic and the rapini
or escarole and sauté for 8 to 10 minutes, or until soft
and wilted. Season with salt and pepper to taste.

Calories: 431
Protein: 46 g
Carbs: 28 g
Fiber: 7 g
Fat Total: 14.5 g

TURKEY TACO SALAD

4 OZ. LEAN, WHITE-MEAT TURKEY, GROUND
¼ CUP CANNED TOMATO SAUCE
1 GARLIC CLOVE, MINCED
2 CUPS CLEANED, CHOPPED ROMAINE LETTUCE LEAVES
3 BLACK OLIVES, SLICED
2 1-IN. SLICES OF AVOCADO
2 TBSP. REDUCED-FAT CHEDDAR CHEESE, SHREDDED
5 TORTILLA CHIPS, CRUSHED
2 TBSP. LOW-FAT, NO-SUGAR RANCH DRESSING
SALT AND PEPPER TO TASTE
NONSTICK COOKING SPRAY

PREPARATION: Heat a nonstick skillet coated with nonstick cooking spray over medium heat. Add the garlic, turkey, and tomato sauce. Simmer for about 5 minutes, or until turkey is cooked through. Meanwhile, pile the lettuce onto a dinner plate and top with the olives, avocado, cheese, and tortilla chips. Spoon turkey onto the salad and drizzle with ranch dressing.

LEAN
DINNERS

Enjoy one NEW Lean Dinner each week in the
Lean Phase.

CHEESEBURGER AND FRIES

5 OZ. GROUND SIRLOIN
1 WHOLE WHEAT HAMBURGER BUN, TOASTED
1 OZ. CHEDDAR CHEESE
2 SLICES OF TOMATO
1 IDAHO POTATO OR SWEET POTATO, CUT INTO 1-IN. STRIPS
CAYENNE PEPPER
MIXED GREEN SALAD
SALT AND PEPPER TO TASTE
NONSTICK COOKING SPRAY

PREPARATION: Preheat oven to 400 degrees. Lay the potato strips on a baking sheet and spray well with nonstick cooking spray. Season the potatoes with salt, pepper, and cayenne pepper. Bake for 20 to 25 minutes, or until they begin to brown and get crispy. Meanwhile, season the ground meat with salt and pepper and form into a patty. Grill or broil burger until desired degree of doneness and melt cheese on top. Serve with mixed green salad.

SHRIMP FRA DIAVOLO OVER LINGUINI

5 OZ. CLEANED SHRIMP, TAILS REMOVED
1 CLOVE OF GARLIC, SLICED
1 CUP JARRED TOMATO SAUCE
1 TBSP. OLIVE OIL
½ TSP. RED PEPPER FLAKES
1 CUP WHOLE WHEAT LINGUINI, MEASURED AFTER COOKING
1 CUP BROCCOLI, STEAMED

PREPARATION: Heat a nonstick skillet over medium heat and add the olive oil, garlic, and red pepper flakes. Sauté the garlic and red pepper until the garlic begins to brown. Then add the tomato sauce and the shrimp and bring mixture to a simmer. After it simmers, reduce the heat and cook until shrimp are pink and cooked through, about 10 minutes. Serve over linguini, with steamed broccoli on the side.

BURN
SNACKS

STRING CHEESE

1 PART-SKIM MOZZARELLA
STRING CHEESE
WITH ½ OF A SLICED
BELL PEPPER

Calories: 86
Protein: 7 g
Carbs: 2 g
Fiber: 1 g
Fat Total: 6 g

RICE CAKE

1 35-CALORIE RICE
CAKE TOPPED
WITH 2 OZ.
OF TURKEY

Calories: 84
Protein: 12 g
Carbs: 7 g
Fiber: 0.5 g
Fat Total: 1 g

LEAN PIGS IN A BLANKET

Calories: 93
Protein: 5 g
Carbs: 8.5 g
Fiber: 1 g
Fat Total: 5 g

½ OF A 6-IN. WHOLE WHEAT LOW-CARB TORTILLA
  (ABOUT 60 CALORIES FOR FULL TORTILLA OR 30 FOR HALF)
½ OF A TURKEY DOG
1 TSP. YELLOW MUSTARD
TOOTHPICKS
NONSTICK COOKING SPRAY

PREPARATION: Spread the mustard on the tortilla, and roll turkey dog in tortilla. Secure turkey dog in tortilla with toothpick, spray lightly with nonstick cooking spray, and cook at 325 degrees for about 12 to 15 minutes, or until tortilla is light and crispy.

Calories: 107
Protein: 6 g
Carbs: 1 g
Fiber: 0 g
Fat Total: 8 g

DEVILED EGGS

1 HARD-BOILED EGG, CUT IN HALF
AND HOLLOWED OUT (RESERVE YOLK)
2 TSP. LIGHT MAYONNAISE
1 TSP. CHOPPED PARSLEY
PAPRIKA FOR COLOR

PREPARATION: Cut the eggs in half and gently scoop out the yolk into a bowl. Mash the yolk and add mayonnaise to get a creamy consistency. Stir in the parsley and scoop the filling back into the egg white. Sprinkle with paprika for color.

GRILLED BBQ STRIPS

2-OZ. CHICKEN BREAST,
  CUT INTO STRIPS
1 TBSP. BBQ SAUCE
SALT AND PEPPER TO TASTE

Calories: 85
Protein: 11.5 g
Carbs: 5.5 g
Fiber: 0 g
Fat Total: 1.5 g

PREPARATION: Season chicken with salt and pepper. Coat with BBQ sauce and grill or broil on both sides until cooked through.

NOVA ON CUCUMBER

2-OZ. NOVA (LOX)
2 TSP. REDUCED-FAT
  WHIPPED CREAM CHEESE
4 CUCUMBER SLICES

Calories: 92
Protein: 11 g
Carbs: 1 g
Fiber: 0 g
Fat Total: 4.5 g

PREPARATION: Spread the cream cheese on the cucumber slices and top with the lox.

STUFFED CELERY

1 STALK OF CELERY (ABOUT 70 CALORIES
  WORTH) FILLED WITH 1-½ OZ.
  OF LOW-FAT SPREADABLE
  CHEESE, SUCH AS ALOUETTE
  OR LAUGHING COW LIGHT

Calories: 79
Protein: 2 g
Carbs: 9 g
Fiber: 1 g
Fat Total: 15 g

COTTAGE CHEESE AND FRUIT

½ CUP 1% COTTAGE
  CHEESE WITH 3
  SLICED STRAWBERRIES

Calories: 91
Protein: 14 g
Carbs: 6.5 g
Fiber: 1 g
Fat Total: 1.5 g

CAPRESE KABOB

Calories: 98
Protein: 6 g
Carbs: 2 g
Fiber: 0.5 g
Fat Total: 7 g

1 ½-OZ. MOZZARELLA BALL

2 CHERRY TOMATOES, HALVED

2 FRESH BASIL LEAVES

1 TBSP. PREPARED PESTO

1 WOODEN OR METAL SKEWER

PREPARATION: Skewer kabobs in this order: cherry tomato, basil, mozzarella, basil, cherry tomato, basil, mozzarella. Serve with pesto.

ALASKAN SEAFOOD LETTUCE CUPS

Calories: 75
Protein: 12.5 g
Carbs: 2 g
Fiber: 0.5 g
Fat: 2.5 g

2 OZ. IMITATION CRAB MEAT

1 TSP. LIGHT MAYONNAISE

½ TSP. WASABI

½ TSP. REDUCED-SODIUM SOY SAUCE

2 LEAVES OF BUTTERLEAF LETTUCE

PREPARATION: Shred the imitation crab and add the mayonnaise, wasabi, and soy sauce. Mix together and wrap in lettuce leaves.

SESAME CHICKEN STRIPS

Calories: 113
Protein: 17 g
Carbs: 0 g
Fiber: 0 g
Fat Total: 2 g

2-OZ. BONELESS, SKINLESS CHICKEN
  BREAST, CUT INTO STRIPS
1 TSP. SESAME SEEDS
1 TBSP. REDUCED-SODIUM SOY SAUCE
SALT AND PEPPER TO TASTE
NONSTICK COOKING SPRAY

PREPARATION: Coat chicken breast in sesame seeds and salt and pepper. Sear in a nonstick skillet coated with nonstick cooking spray, until it is crispy and cooked through. Serve with a side of soy sauce.

Calories: 126
Protein: 10 g
Carbs: 6 g
Fiber: 0.5 g
Fat Total: 6.5 g

MINI SLIDER

2-OZ. LEAN TURKEY BREAST, GROUND
1 TBSP. BBQ SAUCE
1 SLICE OF TOMATO
2 PIECES OF BUTTERLEAF LETTUCE

PREPARATION: Combine the turkey and the BBQ sauce; form into a patty and bake at 350 degrees for 15 minutes, or until cooked through. Place on top of butterleaf lettuce and tomato.

WRAP-AND-ROLL MINI PINWHEELS

½ OF A 6-IN. WHOLE WHEAT LOW-CARB TORTILLA
  (ABOUT 60 CALORIES FOR THE FULL TORTILLA OR 30 FOR HALF)
2 TSP. LIGHT WHIPPED CREAM CHEESE
1 TBSP. ROASTED RED PEPPER, CHOPPED
1 FRESH BASIL LEAF
1 TSP. PARSLEY, CHOPPED
2 SLICES OF TURKEY, ABOUT 1-½ OZ.

PREPARATION: Spread the tortilla with the cream cheese and sprinkle with the chopped parsley. Add the basil and peppers. Top with the turkey meat and roll up tightly. Slice into ½-in. sections.

Calories: 93
Protein: 10 g
Carbs: 9 g
Fiber: 1 g
Fat Total: 3 g

Calories: 180
Protein: 12 g
Carbs: 8 g
Fiber: 1.5 g
Fat Total: 1 g

SMOOTHIE

1 SCOOP WHEY PROTEIN POWDER*

3 TO 4 STRAWBERRIES

½ CUP OF SKIM MILK

4 TO 6 ICE CUBES

FOR A THINNER SMOOTHIE, ADD MORE WATER

PREPARATION: Combine ingredients in a blender.

*Beachbody® has a great Whey Protein Powder. Contact your Coach, or visit **Beachbody.com** or **TeamBeachbody.com** to order.*

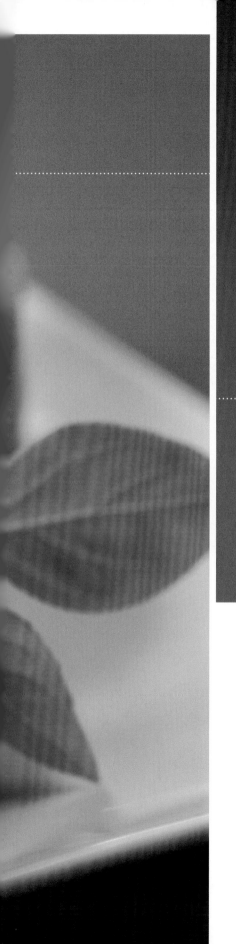

DEVILED TOMATOES

1 ROMA TOMATO, CUT IN HALF AND HOLLOWED OUT

1 HARD-BOILED EGG, DICED

1 TBSP. CELERY, DICED

1 TBSP. ONIONS, DICED

1 TSP. RELISH

1 TBSP. CAESAR DRESSING

SALT AND PEPPER TO TASTE

PARSLEY TO TASTE

Calories: 118
Protein: 7 g
Carbs: 4.5 g
Fiber: 1 g
Fat Total: 7.5 g

PREPARATION: Mix onions, egg, and celery with a small amount of relish and Caesar dressing. Scoop into hollowed-out tomato and garnish with parsley.

SHRIMP
COCKTAIL

3 LARGE SHRIMP, BOILED
2 TBSP. COCKTAIL SAUCE

PREPARATION: Dip shrimp in cocktail sauce.

Calories: 100
Protein: 15 g
Carbs: 6.5 g
Fiber: 0.5 g
Fat Total: 1 g

MINI PIZZA BITES

½ OZ. CHICKEN SAUSAGE, CRUMBLED
½ OZ. PART-SKIM MOZZARELLA CHEESE, SHREDDED
1 TSP. PREPARED PESTO
1/3 OF A ZUCCHINI, CUT ON A BIAS INTO 3 OVAL ROUNDS
1 TSP. PARSLEY, CHOPPED

PREPARATION: Place chicken sausage on top of zucchini slices, mix pesto and mozzarella cheese, and place on top of chicken sausage. Bake at 325 degrees until cheese is melted, about 10 to 12 minutes. When cooked, cool and top with parsley.

PIZZA MARGARITA

½ OF A 6-IN. WHOLE WHEAT LOW-CARB TORTILLA
(ABOUT 60 CALORIES FOR THE FULL TORTILLA
OR 30 FOR HALF)
2 TBSP. MARINARA SAUCE
½ OZ. PART-SKIM MOZZARELLA
CHEESE, SHREDDED
1 TBSP. CHOPPED FRESH BASIL

PREPARATION: Coat tortilla with marinara, top with cheese and basil, and bake in oven at 325 degrees until cheese melts and tortilla is crispy, about 10 to 12 minutes.

Calories: 118
Protein: 7 g
Carbs: 21 g
Fiber: 2.5 g
Fat Total: 3.5 g

TURKEY ROLL-UP

½ OF A 6-IN. WHOLE WHEAT LOW-CARB TORTILLA
(ABOUT 60 CALORIES FOR THE FULL TORTILLA
OR 30 FOR HALF)
½ TBSP. LIGHT MAYONNAISE
½ TBSP. CELERY, DICED FINE
½ TBSP. RED ONIONS, DICED FINE
1 OZ. DELI TURKEY

PREPARATION: Spread the tortilla with the mayonnaise and top with the sliced turkey. Sprinkle with the diced celery and onions. Roll the tortilla very tightly and slice into ½-in. pieces.

Calories: 84
Protein: 7 g
Carbs: 10 g
Fiber: 1 g
Fat Total: 3 g

PUSH
SNACKS

PICK NUTS!

1 OZ. OF NUTS:

20 ALMONDS
Calories: 139
Protein: 5.1 g
Carbs: 4.7 g
Fiber: 2.8 g
Fat Total: 12.2 g

14 WALNUT HALVES
Calories: 185
Protein: 4.3 g
Carbs: 3.9 g
Fiber: 1.9 g
Fat Total: 18.5 g

18 CASHEWS
Calories: 157
Protein: 5.2 g
Carbs: 8.6 g
Fiber: 0.9 g
Fat Total: 12.4 g

30 PEANUTS
Calories: 161
Protein: 7.3 g
Carbs: 4.6 g
Fiber: 2.4 g
Fat Total: 14 g

DARK CHOCOLATE

1-OZ. PIECE (70% PURE ORGANIC COCOA)

Calories: 156
Protein: 1.3 g
Carbs: 17 g
Fiber: 1.5 g
Fat Total: 9 g

BEACHBODY MEAL REPLACEMENT SHAKE

1 SCOOP
1 CUP WATER

VANILLA
Calories: 130
Protein: 14 g
Carbs: 18 g
Fiber: 3 g
Fat Total: 2 g

CHOCOLAT
Calories: 130
Protein: 15 g
Carbs: 15 g
Fiber: 2 g
Fat Total: 2 g

Use ½ cup skim milk for a 170-calorie sha

NUTRITION BAR

**1 HIGH-PROTEIN NUTRITION BAR
WITH AT LEAST 18 GRAMS OF PROTEIN AND
UNDER 300 CALORIES**

*Check out Beachbody's Protein Bars in Café Mocha, Wildberry and NEW Peanut Butter.
Contact your Coach, or visit **Beachbody.com** and **TeamBeachbody.com** to learn more.*

LEAN SNACKS

NUTTY CHOCOLATE

**4 DARK HERSHEY'S KISSES OR OTHER 100-CALORIE PORTION OF DARK CHOCOLATE
DIPPED INTO 1 TBSP. OF ALL-NATURAL PEANUT BUTTER OR ALMOND BUTTER**

> Calories: 96
> Protein: 1.5 g
> Carbs: 11 g
> Fiber: 0.5 g
> Fat Total: 5.5 g

SALAD BAR

Here is a list of salad greens and vegetables that may be used for any lunch or dinner meal. Many of the Fat-Burning meals already include a salad, but when a meal doesn't include a salad, feel free to prepare a salad from the ingredients listed to the right. Just keep in mind that portion sizes still count—even with vegetables. Try to create your "side salads" with 2 cups of vegetables (use low-calorie dressings, such as balsamic vinegar, lemon juice, lime juice, or a bottled dressing with less than 25 calories per serving if needed).

BEST VEGETABLES
TO CHOOSE FROM

DARK LETTUCE LEAVES,
SUCH AS SPINACH, ROMAINE,
AND ARUGULA

CUCUMBER

CELERY

BELL PEPPERS

RADISHES

ONIONS

MUSHROOMS

STRING BEANS

JICAMA

BROCCOLI

CAULIFLOWER

ASPARAGUS

BOK CHOY

CABBAGE

LEAN FOR LIFE MAINTENANCE PROGRAM

After your experience with the Fat-Burning Food Plan, going back to anything that resembles an unhealthy lifestyle is simply out of the question. By now, your body craves healthy meats and fish; crispy, raw veggies; and juicy, succulent fruits—naturally. By now, you have acquired a thorough understanding of how to lead a truly healthy lifestyle. Stay true to these principles; they will never fail to keep you on track. And, if you veer "off the path," don't spend valuable time being hard on yourself. Instead, identify where you took a wrong turn, then go in the right direction!

TRANSITION TO MAINTENANCE

For weight maintenance, try adding 100 calories to your diet for 1 full week. You may add these extra calories by choosing an extra snack, or you may add an additional serving of protein, carbs, or fat to one of your meals. You may find that at this point in your body's transformation, you are craving some additional whole grains. Feel free to add 1 cup/1 serving of a whole grain, such as 1 slice of wheat toast or 1 cup of wheat pasta.

Continue to increase your calories by 100 calories per day each subsequent week, until weight maintenance has been achieved and the weight loss has ceased. For example, if your Fat-Burning calorie level was 1,300 calories, you can start the maintenance stage at 1,400 calories. Then each week increase by 100 calories until you reach your desired weight goal. Generally, 1,600 to 1,800 calories per day results in maintenance for women and 2,000 to 2,200 calories per day results in weight maintenance for men. Keep in mind that calorie needs greatly vary among individuals.

To check out the calorie calculator online, or to expand your diet beyond the recipes within the Fat-Burning Food Guide, log on to **TeamBeachbody.com** for further instruction on choosing healthy foods for weight maintenance.

BE PREPARED

BE PREPARED TO EAT! Try making your meals and your snacks prepacked and ready to go. This is especially helpful when it comes to snacks. **Always carry something in your gym bag or purse,** so you don't get caught off guard when life gets in the way. A handful of almonds, slices of apples in a Ziploc bag, and sticks of string cheese can all save you from "taking the plunge" when your hunger gets the best of you. Try to never "drop" to the point where you get so hungry, your blood sugar truly drops. Snacking is essential to avoid a drop in your blood sugar. Do everything you can to avoid fast food or other unhealthy fixes. You'll only feel worse for the wear soon after eating that stuff.

KNOW YOUR SUPERMARKET STRATEGY

It is so important to go into the supermarket with a plan of action. Getting caught wandering down aisles that hold tempting unhealthy food is never the way to go. Instead, always go to the market with a list in hand so you know exactly what you're after—you'll avoid temptation. Would you really have grabbed that bag of potato chips if you'd had a satiating meal or snack beforehand? And lastly, try to shop around the periphery of the store. When shopping around the outside aisles, you'll find fresh fruits, vegetables, and meats—you'll avoid the center aisles, which are notorious for their high-sugar, high-saturated-fat, and high-calorie food products (even the grocery stores call the center of the store "Death Valley")!

Watch the Healthy Eats & Kitchen Makeover DVD.

ALSO, TRY NOT TO SHOP HUNGRY, WHICH OFTEN LEADS TO BAD DECISIONS!

TIPS FOR
DINING OUT

- Don't go to a restaurant famished. Before going, drink a large glass of water. This will help curb your hunger until your meal is served.

- Decline the bread basket. Ask for fresh veggies instead.

- Fill up on a healthy salad with a low-fat dressing or balsamic vinaigrette as an appetizer, or opt for vinegar and a little olive oil.

- Just because it is not on the menu, don't be afraid to ask for it! Many restaurants will cater to your preferences if you simply just ask.Take control!

- On a similar note, always ask how the entrée is prepared; if it doesn't meet your health standard (e.g., if it's deep fried), inquire about healthy preparation alternatives or order something different. Ask that your meal not be prepared in oil or butter but a cooking spray instead. Request grilled or steamed fish, steamed vegetables, and water with a lemon slice.

- Try to stay away from anything prepared in butter or a cream sauce. If you really want some, simply ask for it on the side so you can control the amount you consume.

- Most restaurant meals come with a vegetable and a starch, like a potato (both carbohydrates). Skip the starches and instead ask for a double serving of steamed vegetables.

- Alcohol inhibits your judgement and is VERY high in sugar. But if you do have an alcoholic drink with a meal, reduce your other carbohydrate intake. Best choices for alcoholic drinks are a glass of wine and light beer. Choose plain liquors, like vodka, whiskey, or gin, with low-calorie mixers, such as club soda, instead of jaeger or kahlua. Avoid mixed or specialty drinks like piña coladas or mai tais—they're loaded with calories and sugar.

- Remember your portions. Portions in restaurants are HUGE. Split a full serving with a friend or ask for half a serving and take the rest home in a doggie bag!

- Lastly, enjoy your night out! Eat slowly, chew slowly, and savor your food! Embrace being in the moment with your friends, family, or mate!

- If you really want dessert, skip the appetizer or reduce the portion of your main course, and again, portions matter.

FREQUENTLY
ASKED QUESTIONS

WHAT DO I DO
WHEN I AM REALLY TIRED?

Research suggests that people who are sleep deprived are more often overweight. This is believed to be caused by two reasons. 1) When we are tired, we look for food as energy, but really, we need sleep, and 2) certain hormones that are released when we are sleep deprived can lead to obesity. Therefore, get your sleep—at least 6 to 8 hours. That said, if you have gone without sleep, try not to use food as your crutch. Drink plenty of fluids, be sure to eat all your meals and snacks, and take a power nap whenever possible.

WHAT DO I DO
WHEN I AM HUNGRY?

During the first 3 to 4 days on the Fat-Burning Food Plan, you may feel hungry. The most important thing you can remember to do is eat every 2 to 3 hours and eat your snacks, so your blood sugar doesn't drop. Sometimes what you assume is hunger is actually frustration that you feel by resisting the temptation to eat when you're not really hungry. When you feel the need to eat, ask yourself what it is you're feeling. Most of the time, you'll find that what you're feeling is in response to habit or emotion. If you're really hungry and it's not time to eat, drink a glass of water and then wait 10 minutes. If you are still feeling hungry, grab a 50- to 100-calorie snack from the snack list, even if it isn't "really" snack time. Limit this 1 extra snack to no more than 1 per day, and only do it when you are truly hungry and not in response to emotional or habitual triggers.

CAN I EAT
LIKE THIS FOREVER?

Heck yes! If you couldn't do this for life, what would be the point? You're going to want to eat this way for the rest of your life (and your life will be longer and better because of it!)!

The first three phases of the Fat-Burning Food Guide are a great way to eat and hit your target weight. While it would not be "unhealthy" to eat this way long-term, you may find that you long for a broader range of foods once you're in the maintenance phase, the Lean for Life Phase. Provided your food choices stay within the same fat, calorie, protein, and carb guidelines, the sky is the limit!

Many people consider going back to their old ways after completing a nutrition plan. That's the dieter's mentality and it's a surefire way to land you right back where you started. Make this your new normal, and you'll feel too good to ever resort back to your old ways. You will be able to allow yourself weekly treats to keep you going for the long haul. Go ahead, enjoy the occasional "no-no," but make room for it in your daily caloric allowance. **Remember, nothing tastes as good as lean feels!**

*Tip: Take a look at Michi's Ladder at **TeamBeachbody.com** to help you broaden your food options.*

HOW MUCH
WEIGHT WILL I LOSE?

People lose weight at varying rates—men and women with more weight to lose will generally lose weight faster. You will likely find that you lose weight quickly for the first 2 to 3 weeks, and then you may hit a plateau for a week or two. But don't give up because weight loss varies. Many of our test participants experienced a leveling off of weight loss during the Push Phase, but the critical muscle development in that phase helps boost the metabolism and sets the stage for dramatic results in the Lean Phase. Keep in mind that you may be losing inches and fat, even when the scale stays the same, that's because you're adding muscle. Use your body's appearance and your body fat caliper—not the scale—as your gauges.

WHAT IF I HAVE TO
GO OFF THE PLAN FOR A VACATION
OR A SPECIAL OCCASION?

Don't think of this as a "diet." Don't feel like you need to put your life "on hold" while following the Fat-Burning Food Plan. Think of this as a new way of life. If you have an upcoming vacation or a special occasion, do the best you can to plan ahead by packing foods and/or calling restaurants ahead of time to find out about the cuisine. With a little creativity and resolve, you can always find a healthy option. Use common sense. Every restaurant offers grilled entrées, salads, and veggies. And lastly, if you do slip a little bit, just get right back on track the next day, with your very next meal. Don't let a slip turn into a slide.

Don't try to do this. Do it! You're worth the effort. You deserve the life that awaits you!